WAVE BOOKS / SEATTLE AND NEW YORK

CHELSEY MINNIS

PUBLISHED BY WAVE BOOKS

WWW.WAVEPOETRY.COM

WAVE BOOKS TITLES ARE DISTRIBUTED TO THE TRADE BY

CONSORTIUM BOOK SALES AND DISTRIBUTION

PHONE: 800-283-3572 / SAN 631-760X

ISBN 979-8-89106-040-1

LCCN 2025043538

CIP DATA IS AVAILABLE UPON REQUEST

FROM THE LIBRARY OF CONGRESS

DESIGNED BY CRISIS

PRINTED IN THE UNITED STATES OF AMERICA

9 8 7 6 5 4 3 2 1

FIRST EDITION

WAVE BOOKS 126

Opera
Fever

A woman threw her fur coat at you
Then someone in the conga line unzips your dress. . .
Don't be so tremendous in bed. . .
That's what you are, isn't it, a little whore. . .
But, I ran to the window anyway with wet eyes and cheeks. . .

And here come the starry whispers
Why do we have to have fun?
We should be beaten over the head with a pink cushion. . .
Are you going to settle everything with a filthy look?
Or give me a smoked-glass ashtray with a big bow on it

It's a lonely party
When you run the knife along the dress strap. . .
And then my happiness depends upon an emerald. . .
So, what is death?
Well, it's a mirrored headboard. . .

I love you with a vileness. . .
And all the nuance of uranium. .
And so what if I'm charming. .
Do they think I want to destroy the world?
And this is why I wear a pearl ring over a black leather glove

I feel a floating agony. . .
An agony like organza. . .
Now are you going to give me what I want
Or will you too die pressed against the door. .
With armfuls and armfuls of mauve veil. . .

Is this a poem or the back of a shovel?
It's a frying pan full of diamonds.
The world is crashing to bits
Come on and say something filthy. .
We're going to die, darling. . .

This is a kind of blackened spring
This is a springtime with dark edges. .
Yes, something is tinglingly wrong!
When you lift your dark eyes like a piano lid
Or a double casket. .

Anyway, I tore up your poems. . .
Well, aren't you glad to see me?
And against all this background I present a doom. .
Now what kind of gentle doom is this?
And some cake frosting for your groin. . .

I wore dingy sequins. . .
I only like very dull sequins. . .
And flesh-toned telephones. . .
And a sudden clang of lens flare. . .
And then you wash up on shore like that

Let's have a fight in the room with the loud wallpaper. . .
I feel as though I'm a rotting flower. . .
I feel an incandescent disgust. . .
My jewels are simmering on my neck. . .
Can you do this to me?

I have all the qualities to make a decent person. . .
And what have I done with them?
I go about all day pursuing jewels, fur, excitement. . .
But be displeased with me, I can't help it
It binds me to you. .

Only you could look so innocent in leather. . .
And so, I wrote you a blazing letter. . .
A letter like a rainbow in autumn. . .
You should be afraid of such a letter
I told you I loved you in the most vile obscenities. . .

I felt very cheap and drunk like cling peaches
And so, I stabbed a curtain.
Life would be like that. . .
And a playpen full of fur coats. . .
And a wall safe behind every painting. . .

You have a loneliness, but it is a masterful loneliness. . .
I don't like a masterful loneliness
Now stand behind me while I play the piano. .
My god, you are a ravishing lion!
Let me be the one to destroy your greatness. .

All right, I love you like a handsome gravedigger. . .
You needn't get hold of yourself
It's just a feral melancholy
That burned a hole in the autumn. .
Darling, I never wrote you the right note. . .

I loved you and then you wore the sequined lapel. . .
Darling, I smashed the lorgnette!
Now I'm going to pour champagne on your face
Then I'll walk on your bed in my shoes. .
Darling, the shoes with bows on them. .

It rained from the chandeliers. . .

So, let's have a drink for breakfast. . .

And pretty soon we were all depressed. . .

I guess you wear a blush suit

A peach shirt, and a brown tie but what could go wrong

The wind blew our hair back the way we liked it

It kind of makes you burst into tears. . .

So, we left it like that

A fantastic argument and then a clumsy kiss

On some cushions in the speedboat. . .

I bit off the rosebud with my teeth. .
Are you going to sing for us?
And so, let's weep on a park bench.
It brings up a feeling like a bulldozer shovel. . .
You see, I thought I couldn't love a man in a flashy tuxedo. . .

Then he comes in wearing his red frock coat. . .
I felt the chevrons of vibration. . .
You know autumn. .
The one with the burned-out center.
Darling, am I hard to love?

And the music opening like a casket. . .
The music like a dripping power line. . .
All the groaning and coughing of silence. . .
Tears slash at my eyes!
And you stand in the rain in a devil costume. . .

A voice like a murderer's gloves. .
Eyes like locked locks. .
I like it when you talk with unexpected softness and mispronounce
    words. . .
I find you to be susceptible. .
It makes me sweat on my mink. . .

Now, sit down and finish your dessert
This is a sheer sleeve that ends in fur
This is a deepening banquet. . .
You had a very glamorous mother who would slap your face after a
 dinner party. . .
One isn't satisfied with fondness. .

Don't hold me so tight. . .
I get bored, darling
I told you I hate yacht parties. . .
Didn't the charm school teach you how to handle this?
You put your bare foot on the tiger's head. . .

So, let's open our gun cases. . .
To find nothing but love notes
These are the pink pumps that I use to walk among the mud puddles. .
Let's see if we can say this any bloodier. .
"This is what it took to console myself."

A sequined emptiness. . .
Like a see-through dress on the bed
Then he covers her mouth while they slow dance. .
The main thing is to whimper and cry at first. . .
And wear chiffon wings in the armpits. .

You have to be plied with drugged gumdrops. .
And wait for the music to fade in like an anesthetic. . .
It's going to hurt, darling!
The feeling of being cut from your shell
I shall have to limp to the bar cart. . .

You lie in bed, lipstick glistening. . .
Then he starts to explain he's a no-good hustler
Do you really want to walk out on a no-good hustler?
So, you pulled the diamond-encrusted lever. .
And it was simply another crate of velvet blindfolds. . .

Do you always sleep with such beautiful eyelids?
On an overstuffed satin chair. .
And then trudge through the leaves like love letters. . .
Darling, you must be roused. .
Darling, you lounge in your melancholy like an alcove. . .

I spit out my food whenever I think of you
So, let's have a shared hearse. .
And then some groaning under the fur coats. .
Let's be very hard on veils. .
Like a dark summer with too many funerals. . .

Don't drown in the fountain in your nightgown!
Under the candy green moonlight
You were meant to be stabbed during a minuet.
Darling, tell me about my wretchedness. . .
And I'll tear off one of your military buttons while I kiss you. .

You have to match your lipstick to your uniform. . .
A romantic push against the vending machine. .
One of us was bad but the other was too.
It was like dying in a bridesmaid dress. . .
There was a special pink dumpster for poems. .

There was a lot of atmospheric loneliness and drones. .
And a hanging bridge between our bedrooms. . .
Sometimes you need that kind of cushion. .
When curtains open and close by themselves
Or a revolver wrapped in a foulard. . .

It was like having a drink in front of you for hours
It made the sequins blur. .
What makes a person lonely?
A statue with closed eyes. .
Or a hairstyle with diamonds in it. . .

He had the same eyes as everybody. .
And a lot of trashy rain. . .
And a dress scraped off like a glaze. .
Now, I see it's a sort of silver wallpaper with seams. . .
So, we drank it out of parfait glasses. . .

I'm sorry I set the checkerboard on fire
I'm a bit sorrier than I thought I'd be. .
Now get me my cigar. . .
And why shouldn't I love a man in harlequin tights?
All you ever gave me was fistfuls of money. . .

Now do we sleep with each other or just put on chenille robes and go
to pieces?
Let's powder our bruises and go dancing. . .
It's simply that we chafed our poor faces with kissing
We tried to have a good time but how could we. .
With all those lovely icebergs melting

It was a friendly kiss wasn't it?
Darling, it was the two-tone sunset. .
It was like you suddenly discovered a bullet wound.
Should I waste it all on a poem?
The burning yachts of my egotism. . .

It was a candy colored autumn
So I went to my room and trembled. .
I could feel an infatuation like a surfeit. . .
And then the hammer of nuance. .
So, I lit a candle for your handsomeness. . .

It's very atmospheric to be in love
There was even a breeze indoors. . .
Let me tell you the awful feeling of happiness when he appears. .
Darling, the clouds slipped out of windows!
You get the feeling of torn-off slipcovers. . .

The song shatters like a dome and falls inward. . .
Or a sledgehammer with a pink bow on
You walked into the pond in your gown. . .
Your headache melted from fondness. . .
The love song preyed upon you like a yawning lion. . .

Now, clear a space in the leaves to lie down and die. .
Have you ever been darkly in love as the leaves fall around you?
Darling, you might be alone in a chair reading a letter. .
Darling, you might be reading that letter for the rest of your life. .
As if the grief is burnt ochre. . .

I tore down the curtains. . .

My nose bled. . .out of love. . .

Please tell me what I can have. .

The springtime forest fires?

Or your dark eyes like the back of a mirror. . .

Can't you console me with your soft voice like mohair?

Your voice like circus squalor. .

Your voice like sequined pants and manure. .

Now, what is the nicest phoniness?

A fabulous grief with quatrefoils and ruffled sleeves?

It was a carnal melancholy
Now shove the love letters in a meat grinder. . .
I was trying to stay alive with a bubbling wound. .
I went mad like a failed weld. .
Darling, I cut open the space suit and died. . .

Look at these letters, they burn beautifully. . .
I must have a fire made entirely of love letters. . .
I must have a revenge like a wound staunched with money. . .
But a very fragile revenge. .
Like a face slap meant to calm you down.

The only way you could talk to each other was to slow dance. .
Three empty champagne glasses on the piano should explain it.
Well, I like this sort of boring nonsense. .
The lake like an abandoned beaded evening bag. . .
And the pink lampshade of sunset. . .

I had several bad thoughts in a row. . .
Like when a carousel slows down. .
And starts to reverse.
Life is not meant to be a burning carnival. .
But a dancefloor that rises on a hydraulic mechanism!

Anyway, I'm going to tear up your poems
Then we can stare at each other like delinquents. .
Now what is death?
Maybe it's a man with doll's eyes. .
And everyone topless in diamond necklaces. . .

Nothing more ominous than a swimming pool. . .
A very serious conversation under a disco ball. .
Well, that's how it was. . .
Drab and exciting. .
Then we just wallpapered over the door

In a big bedroom filled with clouds. . .
A painting of a storm behind his desk. . .
As the wind molds our dresses to our bodies. . .
The smoked lenses of melancholy. .
It was like looking out of eyeholes!

A beautiful woman with smoke coming out of her nostrils. .
Well, aren't you glad to see me?
You know it is a lighter fluid. . .
Encasing the briquette like a slipcover. . .
Darling, what shall I do with my poems?

I'm sick of my pearls.

You take them!

Now let's go mad while someone tosses fake snow over our heads. . .

Is this the same loneliness I ever felt?

Or a soft cream filling of total desolation

I see you suffer under a secret greatness. .

Your voice is like a bed with curtains. . .

Your voice cleaves open like a geode. .

You gave me the very worst dice rolls!

But how gently you untied my bow. .

I like the way he looks at you as if you could really disappoint him. .
Then you talk all night about silence
He sets his gaze and lets it rest. .
He wants you to get under the fur. . .
It's really a fantastic struggle between hopelessnesses. . .

He's the kind of person who can really suffer. .
Meanwhile he got blood all over the banister. . .
I love when you suddenly pour us a drink. .
And someone murmurs to you in a sandstorm. .
All their soufflé of confessions. . .

This poem means nothing to the world. . .
So, chain it to your wrist with a little handcuff. .
I don't object to love. . .
It has a tough little sparkle when you say it.
It sounds like a coffin hinge. . .

I feel a shame like something burning on the stove
I feel a grove-like quiet. . .
And the uneasiness like a mealworm. .
Darling, why am I screaming?
All I wanted was a water trough of pearls. .

I wanted to soil your white vest with tears. . .
I wanted to beat your chest with my fists. . .
How could it have been otherwise?
I was in a mood to hate my gown
I would have eaten my way out of a candy tomb

What should be said in poems. .
A bubbly ambivalence. . .
Or a mirror seen through bullet holes?
You had confetti in your hair. . .
And so, we kept a little gun in our apron. . .

I like it like a crescent-shaped scream. . .

Then you sing the soft part again. .

No matter how gently you set the knife down.

Of course we met at a funeral. .

Everything went dark except one sparkly dress strap.

All your prom dresses went up in flames. . .

That's what made it so lonely. .

The fusion of autumn and satin

And your lipstick glistening. .

Like a reflection on top of a reflection on top of a panoramic view. . .

Apparently, there is a third possibility. . .
Someone could sweet talk you darkly. . .
It would feel wrong not to take it. .
You're a sweet hyena aren't you?
What do you mean it's not the end of the world?

You would walk into a room licking your lips. .
Do you know where that searching ends?
He pulls your skirt up as he talks. .
The forest grows dark pink with fire. .
You better feel like you are falling through the clouds. . .

I don't go around popping balloons with my cigarette. . .
I like to look at you through my drink. . .
I never wrote anything on a mirror with lipstick. . .
I sat at my abandoned poetry booth. .
While autumn burned down like scenery

Do you think poetry is mud on your pillow?
For someone very deserving of flavored syrup. . .
What do you want with a lot of filthy roses?
I loved you like a floating explosive. . .
So I wrote a letter with a broken clasp. .

Shall I go on with my undressing?
You need a poem for your casket. .
And I love it like pulsating icicles. .
I love it like electric belt buckles. .
There I was, mourning in leather. . .

What am I, your dark confectioner?
My obsession like a stained pink bedspread. . .
My obsession like a semi-murder
Darling, I prayed to forget about you and your flawed tuxedos. .
There was some kind of restraint but I didn't know anything about it. .

It was that kind of rotten beauty that made everyone take what they wanted. . .
And that's when I started throwing chairs. . .
I felt that my earrings were trembling. .
During the terrible celibate waltzes. .
My jealousy spread like a ceiling stain. . .

You were pouring gravy down my dress
Darling, feel my forehead. . .
I begin to see your perfection. .
And it's a very fine horror. . .
Like a statue that turns its head

He sings like a heated knife
Then he gives you the lowered eyes. .
And winds up the tension like a coil. .
When he eats the dessert like a scoundrel. . .
My favorite part is his absolutely caramel dishonor. .

I don't know what poems are for
Are they going to help us
What are poems going to do to us
Are they going to stick out like a knife handle?
I walked around that way for a long time

Maybe I just like a man in tights. .
With a voice like a mink trash bag. . .
Darling, feel my forehead. .
It's a crude admission of love. . .
When you dance a waltz without looking at each other. . .

People think everything is beaded gowns and shards of mirror. .
But it's a mirrored shovel. .
It's not just a song but a swelling. . .
It's not just a song but a pressure on my groin. .
Darling, at the end, the wolves licked my hand

Mademoiselle has fainted. . .
What are you? A flimsy railing?
A mirror reflected in a mirror?
Here's the end of the world as promised
And someone flicks their eyes up at you right as they do it. .

There was something so sexual in a flat gaze
She wanted to touch his mauve pants. .
I love when she threw her dress on the grass as a form of melancholy
She ruined him with that happiness. . .
Then he put on a caramel blazer and said goodbye. . .

I behave like a person who has won a prize
But I haven't won a prize
So let's don't have any shaking of heads. .
It was my favorite tuxedo because it was the ugliest. . .
You can't explain that to someone with rosettes in her hair. . .

It was just what I wanted, the whole world. . .
Unfortunately, there were only four chandeliers. . .
Why would you get mixed up in a poetry racket?
A train passed while I thought about it. . .
Then they find you on the floor with your eyes open. .

I love a deserted tennis court. .
The blood-filled teacups of the afternoon. .
While the cigarette burned down
I thought you were the only man who could get me out of this dump. . .
And the dump is my mind. . .

So, he stared at her to make her feel better. .
His eyes looked good against those chair cushions. .
It was like having someone you hated kiss your wounds. . .
You know it came in wavelets. . .
It's a lot of effort just to live like a mouse. . .

The first thing he removes is your glove. . .
And then the roller coaster goes underwater. .
And this is like having your arms pinned.
Darling, it plucks the wire.
And then his eyes lower down on you like talons. .

You didn't even realize you were in love
Everyone was warned about my charm. . .
I decided to spit on their poems. . .
The only thing that comforted me was the fountain. . .
And the drooping rosebuds of autumn. .

But then I wouldn't have known the boxlike loneliness. . .
Or wandered around in a mauve gown. . .
Darling, lower your eyelashes if you get me. .
A sunset behind an old roller coaster
And a lot of smoked glass and flocked wallpaper

It was a tantalizing loneliness. .
And it tied in the back.
How little would be enough. .
If a man with a gaze like a twanging saw. . .
Undid the clasp and walked away. .

Then why not tear each other's sweaters off?
Everyone died with hot pink blood. .
And the sound of a little golden popgun.
She was so hungry for a doorway. . .
We didn't know if it was blood or jam

He was the type to comb his hair afterward.
Well, love wasn't pleasant. .
A man in a mask played an accordion. . .
A woman had to be half nude among the confetti. . .
Except for the ruffle around her neck like a clown. .

It’s too bad she was so vulgar and beautiful. . .

Then she broke the perfume. .

She wore a red coat but she was cold. .

He wanted his usual punishments. . .

But he came in too gently. .

I felt stifled by the elegance. .

So, I rolled around on the carpet to get rid of it. .

You could wash the blood off the plastic curtains. . .

There was no way to stop him from creaking tears out of his eyes. .

So, she braced herself for handfuls of mud

He said he wanted to fuck her on a cliff. . .

You could see the clasp had slipped around. . .

It's difficult to keep impending doom in the front of one's mind. . .

He called her a whore while he tore apart a pink flower.

So, she wore tennis clothes and ran a fever. . .

Darling, it was a single, unsmashed fish tank. .

Well, it had the same effect as a lip scar. .

Anyway, his voice was like four brandies in the tropics

I was on my best behavior that autumn. . .

A poem was pawing at the door. .

Why don't you go float away on a little pink cloud?. . .
Because you are a bad person in monogrammed pajamas. .
Perhaps you are longing to kiss my face?
I felt too detached, so I needed a fur stole
Or a cut-glass highball glass etched with stars. . .

As if I could feel despair in that safari jacket. .
Well, I liked all these beach fevers. . .
So, I avoided the piano for days. .
And then everyone sweated at their hairlines. . .
You could glance at each other on the way to hell, couldn't you?

She was the type to have fun even if she didn't feel like it. . .
She gets that faraway stare like a fawn
Does that mean you're finally smoldering?
The most strange and extraordinary baby. . .
Ever found in a sequined trash pile. . .

It seemed to her there was something terrific wrong with her. .
The semicloseness was killing her. . .
And the sound of the oar. .
She merely pointed her knees toward him. . .
You see, it's only wrong if you do it in the afternoon. . . .

It starts with a bloody piano recital. . .
And a pink cocktail spilled in anger. . .
Everyone was swooning in silence. . .
The car paused with its cloudlike engine. .
And shone a headlight over her dress like a fondle. . .

Then the world starts to move around you in a semicircle
I took the record player and put it by the pool
I couldn't be bothered with any more lovers. .
This was my favorite scene. . .
It all started with him closing the door. .

You could see it was going to be a very deadly war. . .
We were so lonely it was macabre. . .
The other men were like gazelles. . .
An emptiness framed by broken glass.
And a depression like a lot of velvet sandbags. . .

The beauty of a half-open gate. .
As he strolled through the lobby with four men in white suits
And a kind of softly worthless look
The thistles of charisma. . .
Darling, that kind of person can't be mentioned ever again. .

Darling, let's not feel this ruthlessness. .
I wrote you a poem so I could perish with triumph!
The most boring shame of all time
Like a leech on a satin cushion
Or a horribly starry feeling of longing. . .

I like it when the curtains close by themselves. .
Everyone freezes in place, but it's only my boredom. .
My boredom makes me rise like a drone and see the room. . .
If only the mirrors would split us in two. .
Then I'd blow up the world with the very antique control panel of a poem.

Darling, I bed you down for a reason. . .
Darling, your gloominess. . .
You're a very tough brute. .
I love you like leather driving gloves. .
That's why I cracked your skull with a vase of roses. . .

I love you with some kind of terrible pleading. .
And some kind of unpeeled glove
You growled in my ear during the third course. . .
I remember my appalling relief. .
You wore a muscle shirt in the hearse. .

I wanted to deglaze your shoulders of that dress. .
I wanted to murmur into your guts
The bulging pearls around you like a disembowelment. . .
Nothing beguiles me like you and your filth
Or a light shaft on a shoehorn. . .

I only wanted a few slippery drinks. .
To block out the world with tiny mirror balls. . .
The carousel horse with a snarl. . .
Or lipstick smears on the foulard. . .
Then he lit a cigarette right in the middle of a song

I'd never met a little tramp before.
Or a pony with pink ribbons in its mane. .
Darling, put the black stuff on your eyes and let's go out. . .
It was a good time for staring off into the distance. .
Through all the peepholes in the world.

Everyone floated in a tunnel-of-love ride
She died in the tunnel-of-love ride.
Well, she had the misfortune of greatness. .
Part of its charm was that it looked very fake.
Now, let's go down intertwining staircases. .

Then he drove into a field and smoked a cigarette. . .
I like a man in a suit and tie in the forest. . .
Instead of the loneliness, you get a lot of stylish doom. . .
This poem wasn't going anywhere. . .
But there we were with our shadows on the wall. .

It was like standing at the funeral with an umbrella drink. . .
And someone slowly swinging around a pole. .
And it was all a lot of empty lawn furniture. . .
And a lot of stained domes and marbled puddles. . .
And then you began to feel fluorescently ashamed. . .

And then you could die in lace sheets. . .
But first you pull the bellpull. . .
I don't know why we felt so blazingly tired. .
It seemed we were going to be brightly sick. .
And die in tangerine lingerie. . .

Darling, she took off her heavy earrings and picked up the gun. .
It was nobody's fault but it was your fault. .
It's a very muffled click. . .
It gives me a throb in some lobe of the brain. .
It's a very lucky thing to die of oozing serenity. .

Her life came whirling up in her head. . .
And the gazebo began to rotate around her. . .
He gave her his hand to be bitten. .
Or else you cough blood
So, she had to climb onto a motorized clamshell. . .

She was deprived of champagne. .
And a clanging bell of loneliness. . .
She yielded a single diamond brooch like a barnacle. .
This is how she desired to be reviled. . .
Now, let's find our own weakest point and stab it with a fire poker

Nothing is better than walking away from the party into the forest. . .
So we decided to lie down in the living room with our eyes open. .
Could a person be so deserted?
He smoked while he played the piano. . .
If only I had sent you a note that said "come"

I like a tray of drinks on the lawn. . .
And the cloud-darkened sunlight. . .
So, she tore down a web with her hand. .
We all got drunk before dinner. . .
And then decided we were old friends. . .

The rain blew in the French doors, but of course we wanted that. . .
All day long, I begged myself to stop thinking about my obsession. .
My obsession was to smoke a cigarette on a children's carnival ride. .
I planned to be beautiful and deeply absent in a rust evening gown. .
Then stay like that as a cloud darkens the salon. .

It started with her crawling to the door. . .
Then they had to kiss with their tongues. . .
Then the inevitable climbing on and grabbing hold. .
It was like fighting over a ruby or a piece of meat. .
They had to swindle each other out of their bedclothes. . .

It was a mirage of a tableau. . .
And she wore a wool blanket and a diamond necklace. .
She wanted to be fanned while she remembered it. .
She drank drugged fruit drinks to cheer her up. .
Well, everyone had rainbow fevers. . .

And she listened at the door in the nude
I decided to lose my manners. . .
I have a record player in my bathroom. . .
She had a mood like a ripped-up dress. .
So, we got a fur coat out of it. .

ACKNOWLEDGMENTS

For Steve

I would like to especially thank Ruth Tobias for her endless labors and Steve Schmidt for his selfless support. Also a really warm grateful thanks to Joshua Beckman. Also sincere thanks to Heidi Broadhead, David Caligiuri, Jeff Clark!, and all the Wave staff and especially Charlie Wright. Thank you to DH. Thanks to the Giancarlo DiTrapano Foundation for Literature & the Arts and to *Copenhagen*, *ITERANT*, *Washington Square Review*, and *The Poetry Review, UK* for publishing some of the poems that appear in this book.